Table of contents

Service Level Management

IT Infrastructure Library

Central Computer and
Telecommunications Agency
Gildengate House, Upper Green Lane
Norwich NR3 1DW

LONDON: HMSO

© Crown copyright 1989

Applications for reproduction should be made to HMSO

Fifth impression: 1994

ISBN: 0 11 330521 4

Issue: 1.1

This is one of the first books to be published in the IT Infrastructure Library series. At regular intervals, further books will be published and the Library will be completed by 1994. Since many customers would like to receive the IT Infrastructure Library books automatically on publication, a standing order service has been set up. For further details on standing orders please contact:

HMSO Publicity (PU23E3), FREEPOST, Norwich, NR3 1BR
(*No stamp needed for UK customers*).

Until the whole Library is published, and subject to availability, draft copies of unpublished books may be obtained from CCTA if you are a standing order customer. To obtain drafts please contact:

IT Infrastructure Management Services, CCTA, Gildengate House, Upper Green Lane, Norwich NR3 1DW.

For further information on other CCTA products, contact:

Press and Public Relations,
CCTA,
Riverwalk House,
157-161 Millbank,
London, SW1P 4RT.

This document has been produced using procedures conforming to
BSI 5750 Part 1: 1987; ISO 9001: 1987.

Foreword

Welcome to the IT Infrastructure Library module on
Service Level Management.

*In their respective subject areas, the IT
Infrastructure Library publications complement and
provide more detail than the IS Guides.*

*The ethos behind the development of the IT
Infrastructure Library is the recognition that
organizations are becoming increasingly dependent
on IT in order to satisfy their corporate aims and
meet their business needs. This growing dependency
leads to a growing requirement for high-quality IT
services. In this context quality means matched to
business needs and user requirements as these
evolve.*

*This module is one of a series of codes of practice
intended to facilitate the quality management of IT
Services, and of the IT Infrastructure. (By IT
Infrastructure, we mean organizations' computers
and networks - hardware, software and computer-
related telecommunications, upon which
applications systems and IT services are built and
run). The codes of practice are intended to assist
organizations to provide quality IT service in the
face of skill shortages, system complexity, rapid
change, current and future user requirements,
growing user expectations, etc.*

*Underpinning the IT Infrastructure is the
Environmental Infrastructure upon which it is
built. Environmental topics are covered in a separate
set of guides within the IT Infrastructure Library.*

IT Infrastructure Management is a complex subject which for presentational and practical reasons has been broken down within the IT Infrastructure Library into a series of modules. A complete list of current and planned modules is available from the CCTA IT Infrastructure Management Services at the address given in Section 9.

The structure of this module is in essence :

* *a Management Summary aimed at senior managers (Directors of IT and above, senior IT people and in some cases "senior customers" (typically Civil Service grades 3 - 7)*

* *the main body of the text aimed at IT middle management (typically grades 7 to HEO)*

* *technical detail in Annexes.*

*The module gives the main **guidance** in Sections 3 to 5; explains the **benefits, costs and possible problems** in Section 6, which may be of interest to senior staff; and provides information on **tools** (requirements and examples of real-life availability) in Section 7.*

CCTA is working with the IT industry to foster the development of software tools to underpin the guidance contained within the codes of practice (ie to make adherence to the module more practicable), and ultimately to automate functions.

If you have any comments on this or other modules, do please let us know. A comment sheet is provided with every module; please feel free to photocopy the comment sheet or to let us have your views via any other medium.

Thank you. We hope you find this module useful.

Synopsis

Service Level Management is the process of managing the quality of delivered IT service according to a written agreement or 'contract' agreed between the users and the IT Services Section. This contract defines the responsibilities placed on these parties and in particular binds the IT Services Section to offer an agreed quality and quantity of service so long as the users constrain the demands they place upon the service within agreed limits. The relationship between the IT Services Section and its users is thereby put onto a formal, business-like footing, rather like that between a retailer and customers. When invoked in conjunction with charging for the use of the IT Services, as described in the IT Infrastructure Library **Cost Management** module, Service Level Management forms a basis for running the IT Facility as a 'business' or a profit centre.

This module guides organizations through the processes involved in setting up and maintaining Service Level Management. It describes the benefits which include: more clearly defined terms of reference for the IT Services Section; ways of measuring the performance of IT Services Management; the establishment of an agreed, common understanding between the IT Services Section and the users; better, more consistent IT Service quality, matched to organizations' evolving business needs and user requirements. Service Level Management can be used as a basis for an IT Quality Improvement Programme ("do it right first time and then, without additional cost, do it better"). Service Level Management thus addresses organizations' requirements for a quality IT facility, matched to business needs and user requirements as they evolve - a requirement that is becoming increasingly important as IT becomes more pervasive, and dependency on it grows.

1. Management summary

"If you aim at nothing, that is usually what you hit "

(Anon)

The meaning of this quotation is well understood in the business field and the practice of setting targets, monitoring them closely, and then making any necessary adjustments is well established. This guide shows how to apply these same principles to IT Infrastructure Management.

Service Level Management is the process of managing the quality and quantity of delivered IT service according to a written agreement or 'contract' between the users and the IT Services Section. This contract defines the responsibilities placed on these parties and in particular binds the IT Services Section to offer an agreed quality of service so long as the users constrain the demands they place upon the service within agreed limits. The relationship between the IT Services Section and its users is thereby put onto a formal, business-like footing, rather like that of a retailer and customers. When invoked in conjunction with charging for the use of the IT Services, as described in the IT Infrastructure Library **Cost Management** module, Service Level Management forms a basis for running the IT facility as a 'business' or a profit centre.

This module guides organizations through the processes involved in setting up and maintaining Service Level Management. It provides guidance on the maintenance and reviewing of Service Level Agreements(SLAs) and on the maintenance of service quality in the face of change. It clearly points out the dependency of Service Level Management on other infrastructure management processes such as Capacity Management, Availability Management, Configuration Management, Change Management and Problem Management, and directs the reader to other IT Infrastructure Library modules where they require advice and guidance on these processes. The module describes the benefits which include: more clearly defined terms of reference for the IT Services Section; ways of measuring the performance of IT Services Management; the establishment of an agreed, common understanding between the IT Services Section and the users; better, more consistent IT Service quality, matched to organizations' evolving business needs and user requirements.

Service Level Management can be used as a basis for an IT Quality Improvement Programme (*"do it right first time and then, without additional cost, do it better"*).

Service Level Management thus addresses organizations' requirements for a quality IT facility, matched to business needs and user requirements as they evolve - a requirement that is becoming increasingly important as IT becomes more pervasive, and dependency on it grows.

The organization's senior Executive and Business Managers must be aware of the SLAs and their implications, particularly with regard to quality (the effect that poor service quality has on the efficient and effective running of the organization's business) and cost (a long-term cost saving is likely in most cases).

For Service Level Management to be fully effective adequate support tools are very important. Section 7 describes the types of tool required, and gives examples of those currently available. It also gives brief details of work currently being undertaken by CCTA to stimulate the development of new tools, and enhancements to existing tools, to provide further assistance.

Suggested contents for a Service Level Agreement are given at Annex A, and a skeleton Service Level Agreement is provided at Annex B. This provides a standard model upon which Departments can base their own agreements. **This model will also be used as a basis for support tools and training courses which CCTA will be developing in the future. It is therefore recommended that organizations that may wish to use these facilities should use this standard format for their own agreements.**

While recognizing the 'cultural' difficulties that may be encountered in some organizations in converting to an arms- length contractually based relationship between the IT Service Providers and users, the module nevertheless strongly recommends that all organizations implement Service Level Management as soon as possible.

The organization of IT Service provision on the basis of SLAs is likely to be beneficial in all cases. It should not be seen just as a stepping stone to Facilities Management (FM). Service Level Management is however relevant to FM - SLAs will form a basis for most FM contracts. The IT Infrastructure Library module on **Managing Facilities Management** explains the relevance of Service Level Management to the control of externally-provided IT Services.

2. Introduction

2.1 Purpose

The purpose of this module is to provide guidance to organizations on how to justify and establish a Service Level Management function, and the procedures that will be necessary to plan for, implement and run Service Level Management. The skeleton Service Level Agreement(SLA) at Annex B provides a basis upon which organizations can formulate their own agreements.

2.2 Target readership

This module of the IT Infrastructure Library is aimed at Directors of IT, and the IT Services Manager and his staff who contribute towards the provision of IT services. The IT Services Manager is the head of the IT Services Section, and has overall responsibility for service quality. Typically his peer managers are the Applications Development Manager(s) and the Administration and Finance Manager(s), and they are all responsible to the organization's Director of IT (see Figure 6 on page 23).

This module has particular relevance for those involved in negotiating, reviewing and managing SLAs. Some of the information will also be relevant to managers of User Branches, or their representatives. It will help them establish what they should look for and expect of their IT services, in terms of quality and support, and the role they should play to influence this.

2.3 Scope

Service Level Management is the process of managing the quality and quantity of delivered IT service, in the face of changing business needs and user requirements, according to a contract agreed between the users and the IT Services Section. Service quality is defined with respect to service availability, reliability, performance, capacity for growth, levels of support provided to the users, contingency planning, and optionally, security. The quality of service is also defined in terms of some minimum acceptable level of satisfactorily delivered system functionality, as outlined in Annex G. Service quantity is defined in terms of scheduled hours and throughput of work processed.

Figure 1 shows the formal interrelationship of the Service Level Manager (who is the person in the IT Services Section responsible for negotiating and administering the SLAs), the users and the Service Level Agreements in a very simplified form. The users and the Service Level Manager(s) - there could be more than one of them - contract to an SLA in respect of the services that run on the IT Infrastructure / System.

Figure 1:
User / Service Level
Manager relationship

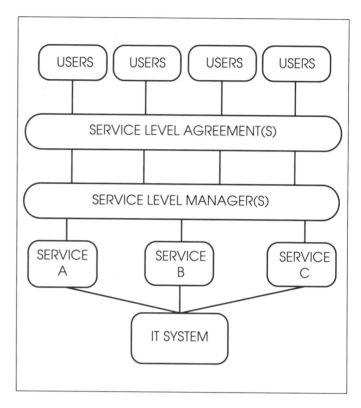

This guide covers all aspects of why such SLAs are necessary, and how they should be negotiated and managed.

Figure 2 shows examples of the additional relationships (often formal contracts) between the IT Services Section and various suppliers and maintainers of IT Infrastructure components, for the essential elements necessary to meet the required service quality. A single contract may cover all elements of service quality from one supplier.

The user - Service Level Manager - supplier relationship is very similar to that between a customer - retailer - wholesaler, in that the service offered by a retailer to his customers is dependent to a great extent on the service he gets from his wholesaler. The Service Level Manager must accept responsibility for any problems the user encounters - in the same way that a retailer is legally obliged to deal with customer problems, without merely fobbing them off to the wholesaler.

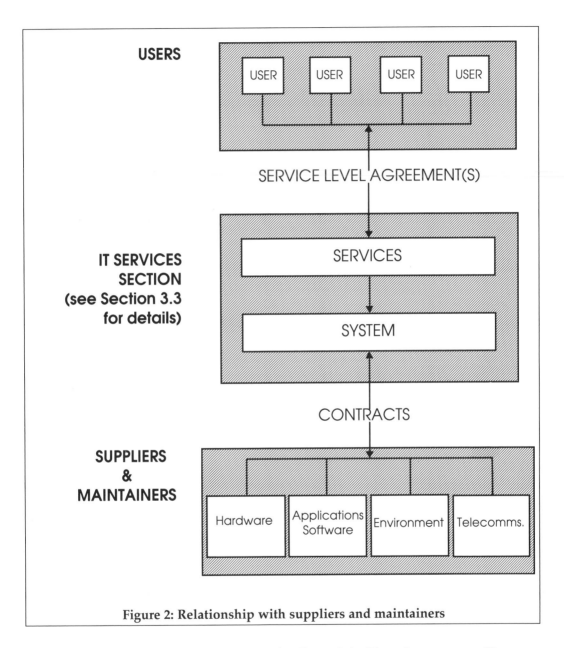

Figure 2: Relationship with suppliers and maintainers

As indicated in Figure 2 the IT services run on an IT System/Infrastructure. It is essential that the contracts with the suppliers and maintainers of the IT Infrastructure components fully underpin the user requirements (eg a 2 second response time to the user will not be possible if the network is incapable of achieving better than 3 seconds).

This means that these contracts must, where applicable, cover the following elements of service quality:

* Delivery and Acceptance Dates

* Availability

* Reliability

* Performance

* Functionality

* Security.

It is important to remember that even if applications software is developed in-house, the quality elements listed above must still be managed. It is therefore recommended that some form of formal agreement is made with the application developers and maintainers to cover the following:

* applications development:

    - delivery dates

    - reliability & availability

    - performance

    - capacity requirements

    - functional acceptance criteria

* application maintenance/support

    - a support agreement, primarily covering time to fix faults according to their severity

    - Help Desk diagnostic scripts

and optionally, depending on the delegated authority of IT Services to handle faults in applications:

* procedures for fixing functional, performance or security problems

* support documentation.

Although such an in-house agreement will obviously not be legally binding or enforceable, it will allow the organization's senior management to establish where the fault lies if the applications developers or maintainers default on the agreement.

In addition to defining supply and maintenance contracts, the IT Services Section is responsible for the management activities necessary to ensure on-going maintenance of the service quality. Section 2.5 lists separate modules which explain the contractual criteria and ongoing management activities that are necessary to underpin Service Level Management.

Where the provision of IT Services is contracted out to a Facilities Management supplier, Figure 3 shows how the Facilities Management agreement can encompass the separate contracts between the IT Services Section and the various suppliers. The Facilities Management provider assumes day-to-day responsibility for these. The Service Level Manager's role will change accordingly. A separate module is available covering the control and management of Facilities Management.

2.4 Context

This book is one of a series of modules issued as part of the IT Infrastructure Library. Although this module can be read in isolation, it should be used in conjunction with other IT Infrastructure Library modules. Section 2.5 lists the other modules that are most relevant.

Figure 3:
Facilities Management

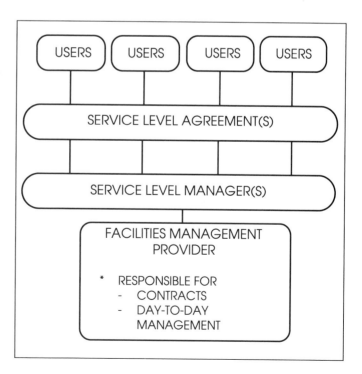

2.5 Related guidance

The following IT Infrastructure Library modules have particular relevance:

The **Availability Management** and **Third Party & Single Source Maintenance** modules describe the contracts and conditions pertaining to reliability and availability for the supply and maintenance of IT service components that are necessary to underpin the SLAs. The Availability Management module also covers ongoing management activities needed to ensure that reliability and availability levels specified in the SLAs are maintained.

The **Capacity Management** module describes the processes that will ensure that adequate capacity is always available to meet required performance needs, in the face of changing user needs and business requirements.

The **Configuration Management, Change Management** and **Problem Management** modules explain the important daytoday management processes that are necessary in order to maintain high quality IT services in the face of change.

The **Help Desk** module gives guidance on the management of User Help Desks and on the processes that are required to underpin User Help Desks. The quality of Help Desk support to users is often covered in SLAs.

The module **Liaison Between IT Service Providers and Users** gives guidance on other related aspects of the relationship between the IT Service providers and their users.

The **Vendor Management** module gives guidance on managing the IT Division's relationship with IT Infrastructure component suppliers and maintainers. Vendors actions may be critical to the successful provision of quality IT Services and therefore to the success of the SLAs.

For Service Level Management to be fully effective it is recommended that some form of charging, or notional charging is made for the services provided. The **Cost Management** module describes all aspects of costing and charging for IT services.

2.6 Definitions

Service Level Management is the process of negotiating, defining, contracting, monitoring and reviewing the levels of user service, that are both required and cost justified.

This process includes:

*   User Management (or a nominated representative) and IT Services Management reaching agreement on the Service Level Requirements transformation of these requirements into Operational Requirements (ORs) and contracts with suppliers and maintainers as shown in figure 2

*   documenting the service level requirements in formal Service Level Agreements (SLA)

*   monitoring, reporting and reviewing the achieved service levels

*   initiation of actions to overcome problems identified in meeting the service levels.

*   ensuring SLAs are regularly updated to reflect changing business needs and user requirements.

A **Service Level Agreement** is the written agreement or "contract" between the users and the IT Services Section, which documents the agreed service levels for an IT service. Typically it will cover: Service Hours, Service Availability, User Support Levels, Responsiveness, Restrictions, Functionality, and Contingency. It may also include Security and Accounting Policy. A Service Level Agreement between users and an internal IT Services Section obviously cannot be made legally binding. When the IT facility is being provided by an FM supplier however, SLAs become part of the legal contract of service between the Department and the Facilities Management provider. Please refer to the IT Infrastructure Library module **Managing Facilities Management** for further details of managing FM.

A **User** is anyone who uses the IT service, including IT development staff. The roles of other people involved are defined in sections 3.3, 4.3 and 5.3.

A **Service** may range from access to a single software application program, to use of one or more global facilities (eg a Transaction Processing System, a suite of Batch programs or a Print System).

Availability is the proportion of time that the service is **actually** available for use by the user, within the agreed service times. An SLA includes agreed service times.

This is calculated as follows:

$$\% \text{ Availability} = \frac{\text{Available Time}}{\text{Agreed Service Time}} \times 100$$

(eg if the service is available for 39 hours within a 40 hour agreed service time period, availability = ((39/40) x 100) = 97.5%).

Note! A service may be available to one or more users at the same time that it is unavailable to others, due to component failure. Each user will therefore have his/her own perception of availability (see Annex A for details of how availability should be represented in the SLA).

Demand Management is the term used to describe a set of techniques for influencing the likely demand for computer resources at any specific time (eg charging less during the off-peak times to encourage use, or implementing limits or restrictions to discourage or prevent use).

A **Service Failure**, for the purpose of this module, is where the whole or part of a service is unavailable, or perceived as unavailable by any user, or where the service falls below an acceptable level of functionality. This could be due to a program failure or data corruption. Poor response times or severe usability problems could render the service unavailable.

User Response Time is usually expressed as "the time between pressing the send key to initiate an interaction and the display at the terminal of the first character of the response".

Note! In some circumstances, however, the ability to proceed with productive work may depend on the whole screen being filled and the keyboard becoming unlocked for use. This should be considered at the time an SLA is formulated and, if necessary, specified in the agreement.

Throughput is the total amount of work processed by the system, per unit time, in the period covered by the agreement. This may be expressed in a number of ways, for example, the number of transaction level interactions in a week; the number of records accessed or modified per hour.

2.7 Standards

The following standards are applicable in the area of Service Level Management:

CCTA SSADM - Structured Systems Analysis and Design Method

SSADM is the standard systems analysis and design method used for applications development in Government. For new and existing applications, SSADM provides information on user requirements which can be incorporated in SLAs.

ISO 9000 series, EN29000 and BS5750 - Quality Management and Quality Assurance Standards

The IT Infrastructure Library modules are being designed to assist their adherents to obtain third-party quality certification to ISO9001. Organizations' IT Directorates may wish to be so certified and CCTA will in future recommend that Facilities Management providers are also certified by a third-party certification body, to ISO 9000. Such third-parties should be accredited by the NACCB, the National Accreditation Council for Certification Bodies.

3. Planning for Service Level Management

Guidance on the benefits that will result from Service Level Management is given in Section 6.

Once it is agreed to introduce Service Level Management, the first step must be to appoint or designate a Service Level Manager, who will be responsible for negotiating and managing the Service Level Agreement(s). This post will normally be within the IT Services area (see section 3.3 for further details and Annex C for a sample Job Description).

3.1 Procedures

Once appointed, the Service Level Manager must carry out the following planning tasks.

3.1.1 Existing services

Where Service Level Management is being introduced for existing services **it is recommended that all services running on the same system are considered at the same time, so that the impact of each service on the others can be fully taken into account.** The following steps must be undertaken:

.1 Mount awareness campaign

Prior to detailed discussions with interested parties, an awareness campaign must be mounted in order to gain the commitment of users, IT Services Personnel and Senior Management. It is essential that everyone is made aware of why Service Level Management is being introduced, what the benefits will be, how they will be affected, and what will be required of them.

This campaign could take the form of circulars, discussion papers, seminars, or a combination of all these. CCTA intend to develop training courses which will be of benefit in this area. Current details are available from the CCTA branch shown in section 9.

.2 Catalogue existing services

At the outset it is essential that the Service Level Manager has a full understanding of the services offered, their characteristics, and all relevant information about the users. To achieve this, all service characteristics must be documented in a Service Catalogue. This must include details of how to identify the service during running, and for monitoring purposes. An example Service Catalogue document is given at Annex D.

Part 1 of this document should be used to gather information from within the IT Division about existing services.

Part 2 should be used to add users' Service Level Requirements, and may also be used to include existing service achievements (in practice organizations may have to tailor this part of the document to suit their own needs). Ideally this information should be stored in some form of spreadsheet or database package.

Where applicable, SSADM-based implemented system descriptions and specifications are a valuable source for the information for part 1 of the Service Catalogue.

**.3 Plan the user/
agreement structure**

A 'Service' is an IT facility to which particular service levels, or sets of service levels, will apply. The Service Level Manager must define his IT 'Services' before starting discussions with users. A service may range from access to a single software application program, to use of one or more global facilities (eg a Transaction Processing System, a suite of Batch programs or a Print System). However the mapping of users onto particular SLAs must be negotiated. The Service Level Manager must produce a plan giving proposals of how the users will be grouped together, the scope of each agreement, and who the signatories will be, as a basis for discussions with the users.

.4 Negotiate with users

The first step must be to agree the structures mentioned at 3.1.1.3 above with the users. This is a very important element of the planning and may be time consuming and iterative (see Annex E for further guidance on these structures).

When this is completed the contents and values to be included in each agreement should be planned in conjunction with the users (see Annex A for guidance on SLA contents). In many cases the levels of service currently offered (measured, say, over the previous three months) could act as a starting point, providing they are acceptable. Where they are not, target service level requirements must be planned. In any event the effect of future workload changes on service levels must be taken into account from the outset. Care must be taken to ensure that these are realistic and achievable. Where service improvements are requested which demand capital investment or additional ongoing costs (eg additional staff, tighter maintenance contracts) organizations must decide whether they are prepared to make this investment. In many cases there will be a net saving as a result of improved user productivity. See Section 6 for example calculations.

The Service Level Manager must act as a focal point for evaluating the impact and cost of users' service level requirements. Modelling tools will have to be used to predict capacity and configuration reliability and availability requirements to support these service levels. This is an iterative process leading to agreed service requirements only when all parties are satisfied that a correct balance between requirements, and the costs and complexity of meeting them, has been reached. Ongoing running costs must be considered in addition to initial capital costs. From IT Services, the Availability , Capacity and Cost Management functions should all be directly involved alongside the Service Level Manager. See the IT Infrastructure Library modules on these subjects for further information.

In order to guarantee agreed levels of service it will be necessary to set limits on the volume of work to be accommodated. These limits must be agreed with the users, and a policy must be established on what action to take if they are exceeded. If a user who exceeds a limit is only likely to degrade his/her own level of service (eg where a machine is dedicated to one user/workload) then it may be sufficient to make any limits advisory only. If however the effect is likely to impact upon other users, and other SLAs, then restrictions must be imposed.

If it is desirable to allow some flexibility within these limits it may be sufficient to set just a total maximum number for all transactions and allow the users to decide which transactions to run within this limit. If however the transaction types vary in resource requirements it is necessary to decide upon a 'standard transaction' and then equate all others to it, in terms of resources required (eg a purchase transaction might be designated as the 'standard', and a sales transaction may equate to 1.5 standard transactions; given a total limit of 15000 standard transactions the user could then decide whether to run 15000 purchase transactions, or 10000 sales transactions, or any combination of each up to the limit). Analysis of transactions in this way will have to be done in conjunction with the Capacity Manager, using techniques described in the Capacity Management module.

Suggested contents for a Service Level Agreement are given at Annex A, and a skeleton Service Level Agreement is provided at Annex B. This provides a sound model upon which organizations can base their own agreements.

.5 Review underpinning contracts

The Service Level Manager must review the underpinning supply and maintenance contracts, depicted in Figure 2, to ensure they are capable of supporting the required levels of service. Where contracts are not considered sufficiently stringent to support the users' service level requirements, consideration must be given to re-negotiating these contracts. This is likely to involve additional costs. The Service Level Manager and users must jointly decide whether these costs to the organization are justifiable, and if so, put a case to senior management, or amend the service level requirements accordingly. Guidance on cost justification methods is included in Section 6.

.6 Plan service monitoring improvements

In order to manage service levels they must be measurable. Monitoring facilities must therefore be reviewed and plans made for any enhancements. This should be done in conjunction with the Availability, Operations, Capacity, Help Desk and Problem Management functions which are responsible for supplying the information on a day-to-day basis (see Annex F for guidance on those elements to be monitored). Ideally the monitoring tools used must be set-up in such a way that individual agreements can be easily monitored without the need for time consuming analysis of the total system statistics. Some tools allow a limited amount of tailoring in order to achieve this. Section 7 describes some tools currently available, and the efforts being made by CCTA to influence their improvement.

.7 Ensure supporting processes are adequate

A major purpose of Service Level Management is to maintain existing service levels in the face of changing demand. To achieve this fully a number of supporting processes must exist (see Section 3.2). Separate modules are available covering each of the processes. Plans must be made to install, or improve, these processes where necessary.

.8 Plan service improvement program

Service Level Management provides a basis for improving service quality and quantity, at minimum cost. Plans should be made for such a service improvement programme. See Section 5.1.6 for further details. The supporting processes described in Section 3.2 must be in place.

.9 Consider accounting policy

Consideration must be given to notional charging, if this does not already occur. This improves cost consciousness which allows comparisons and promotes better management of resources (see Section 7 for details of accounting tools). The user is able to compare resources used in the reporting period with previous relevant periods and, after taking into account the nature of usage and relative business levels etc, may be able to identify if computer resources are being used effectively and efficiently. Trade-offs of service levels versus costs may be possible. Details of any notional charging must be included in the SLA.

Consideration should also be given to a policy for dealing with capital costs. If for example additional equipment is required in order to accommodate the requirements (including service levels) of a new user on an existing configuration, who pays? Should the total cost be borne by the new user, or shared amongst all users? This sort of issue should be planned for and a policy established and agreed. A separate module on **Cost Management** gives guidance on such issues.

.10 Plan for growth

It is a fact of life that demands for IT services tend to grow. Plan to maintain service levels in the face of workload growth. This requires that growth projections are obtained at regular intervals and capital investment plans are made to reflect these projections. Investment in new capacity must in all cases be cost justified. Organizations should also consider the scope for demand management - for which charging can be a 'weapon'. Further information is available in the IT Infrastructure Library **Capacity Management** module. See also section 5.1.7 of this module.

.11 Plan review procedures

Plans must be made for regular service reviews, and reviews of the SLAs (see sections 5.1.4 and 5.1.7 for details).

.12 Establish priorities

There will be occasions when IT staff operating or supporting the system will need to know the priority levels of each service (eg when running a degraded system, or recovering from a system break). This information may be required at very short notice. The Service Level Manager must therefore establish this information in advance.

This is not possible by simply dealing with individual users, as each will regard their own service as a high priority. The assessment must therefore be made at an overall business level, with services being allocated priorities in order of their importance to the organization's business.

Senior Business Management involvement is therefore essential. Details of these priorities should be included within the SLAs, but may be documented separately if very volatile or sensitive.

3.1.2 New or modified services

For ease of reference, some of the text in section 3.1.2 is repeated from 3.1.1. We apologise to those readers who are working through from beginning to end for this repetition.

Figure 4 shows the steps that must be taken when applying service level management to a new or modified service.

In such cases the planning of service level management must be an integral part of the service planning process and the importance of involving the Service Level Manager during all stages of the planning cycle cannot be over emphasized.

An awareness campaign, as described in 3.1.1.1, will be needed to obtain backing for Service Level Management. Having educated IT Division staff and users to recognize the importance of Service Level Management, the Service Level Manager must plan the User/Agreement structure as described in 3.1.1.3. He must then:

.1 Establish users' initial service level requirements

Where SSADM is used, these requirements are documented in the Problems and Requirements List. Where SSADM is not used, or the documented information is insufficient, the Service Level Manager must speak with the users and/or Systems Analysts to establish these requirements.

.2 Evaluate and agree service level requirements

The Service Level Manager must act as a focal point for providing technical assistance to the systems analyst in evaluating the users' service level requirements and formulating proposed IT systems to meet them. This activity will include the use of modelling tools to establish the technical feasibility and the cost of each proposal. This is an iterative process leading to agreed service requirements only when all parties are satisfied that a correct balance between requirements, and the costs and complexity of meeting them, has been reached. Ongoing running costs must be considered in addition to initial capital costs.

**Figure 4:
Implementing SLM for a
new or modified service**

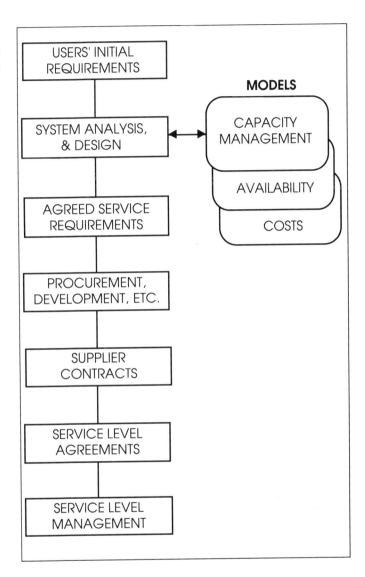

From IT Services, the Availability, Capacity and Cost
Management functions should all be directly involved
alongside the Service Level Manager. See the IT
Infrastructure Library modules on these subjects for further
information.

It is against these requirements that any new system will be
procured and implemented.

In order to guarantee agreed levels of service it will be necessary to set limits on the volume of work to be accommodated. These limits must be agreed with the users, and a policy must be established on what action to take if they are exceeded. If a user who exceeds a limit is only likely to degrade his/her own level of service (eg where a machine is dedicated to one user/workload) then it may be sufficient to make any limits advisory only. If however the effect is likely to impact upon other users, and other SLAs, then restrictions must be imposed.

If it is desirable to allow some flexibility within these limits it may be sufficient to set just a total maximum number for all transactions and allow the users to decide which transactions to run within this limit. If however the transaction types vary in resource requirements it is necessary to decide upon a 'standard transaction' and then equate all others to it, in terms of resources required (eg a purchase transaction might be designated as the 'standard', and a sales transaction may equate to 1.5 standard transactions; given a total limit of 15000 standard transactions the user could then decide whether to run 15000 purchase transactions, or 10000 sales transactions, or any combination of each up to the limit). Analysis of transactions in this way will have to be done in conjunction with the Capacity Manager, using techniques described in the **Capacity Management** module.

Suggested contents for a Service Level Agreement are given at Annex A, and a skeleton Service Level Agreement is provided at Annex B. This provides a sound model upon which Departments can base their own agreements.

.3 Ensure underpinning contracts are planned and negotiated

The Service Level Manager must ensure that the underpinning supply and maintenance contracts depicted in Figure 2 (Page 5) are planned and negotiated. These contracts must be sufficiently stringent to support the service levels in the agreed Service Level Requirements.

.4 Consider the impact on existing services

Where new or modified services are to run alongside existing services, **the Service Level Manager should apply Service Level Management to the existing services as well as the new ones**, if this has not already been done. The existing services will be affected by, and affect the new services and the users of existing services must therefore be consulted to ensure their interests are not jeopardized. The

Capacity, Availability and Operations Managers in particular must be consulted to establish the likely extent of the impact.

.5 Agree necessary amendments to service level requirements

As the service develops through the various stages of design, procurement, development, implementation etc, a number of system modifications may result in amendments to the agreed service requirements. This process will involve iterative consultations with the users.

.6 Other steps

Other steps that must be taken are the same as for existing systems (see sections 3.1.1.6 to 3.1.1.12).

3.1.3 Contingency planning

Organizations must consider how to provide an IT service of acceptable quality in the event of disaster striking the IT infrastructure. Advice on this is given in the IT Infrastructure Library **Contingency Planning** module. If it is impossible to plan to run a normal service on a standby system the SLA should include details of the restricted services that will be provided. In practice it is recommended that for each SLA that is in existence an emergency service SLA is drawn up.

3.2 Dependencies

The Service Level Manager must take care not to sign-up to over ambitious Service Level Agreements too early. For Service Level Management to be fully effective the contracts described in Figure 2 must be in place and fully underpin the SLAs. In addition a number of supporting processes need to be established in advance (if they do not already exist).

It is essential that well ordered mechanisms are established for at least the following:

* Managing changes

* Dealing with problems

* Planning and managing capacity

* Planning and managing availability

* A user-support function (preferably a Help Desk).

Figure 5 shows the recommended supporting processes. Separate modules are available covering each of these. **Apply these processes to the whole IT system on which the service(s) concerned are to run.**

AVAILABILITY MANAGEMENT	OPERATIONS MANAGEMENT	CAPACITY MANAGEMENT
NETWORK MANAGEMENT	**SERVICE LEVEL MANAGEMENT**	HELP DESK
CONTINGENCY PLANNING		PROBLEM MANAGEMENT
* SECURITY MANAGEMENT	CHANGE MANAGEMENT	CONFIGURATION MANAGEMENT

* required if SLAs cover Security

Other dependencies will include adequate monitoring and modelling tools, and a high degree of Senior Management, User and IT Services personnel commitment (see section 3.1.1.1 for details of how this is achievable).

3.3 People

3.3.1 IT Services Manager

The IT Services Manager is the head of the IT services section, and has overall responsibility for service quality. Typically his peer managers are the Applications Development Managers and the Administration and Finance Manager, and they are all responsible to the organization's Director of IT (see Figure 6). The IT Service Manager's staff are responsible for the activities shown in Figure 5. These staff include the managers listed in section 3.3.6 to 3.3.9.

Due to the composite nature of SLAs the IT Services Manager must play a major role in the negotiation and finalization of SLAs - even if much of the work is delegated to a 'Service Level Manager'.

3.3.2 Users

Users perform a major role in defining service requirements. A lot of assistance is required from the Service Level Manager and systems analysts in helping formulate and articulate these requirements, and in evaluating the feasibility and cost of meeting them.

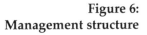
Figure 6:
Management structure

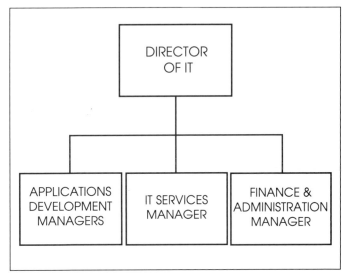

3.3.3 Service Level Manager

Either the IT Services Manager, or one of his/her staff (depending on the scale of the installation), should be designated as 'Service Level Manager'. The Service Level Manager is responsible for both negotiating and managing the Service Level Agreements (see Figure 1 for structure details).

A job description for this post is given at Annex C. He/she must have sufficient authority within the organization to negotiate with and relate to senior user and IT Managers. It is likely therefore that the post must be at least Civil Service SEO level, and it may need to be at a higher grade.

In large installations the Service Level Manager post will need to be full-time, particularly during the initial period when agreements are first negotiated, and some support staff may also be required. Where large numbers of services exist, more than one Service Level Manager may be needed.

In small installations the Service Level Manager role may not be justifiable as a full-time job, and should be combined with another role(s), possibly that of IT Services Manager.

3.3.4 Senior management

The organization's senior Executive and Business Managers must be aware of the SLAs and their implications, particularly with regard to cost, and the effect that poor service quality has on the efficient and effective running of the organization's business (low productivity, poor morale and lack of confidence in the IT Division among IT service users).

3.3.5 Signatories to SLAs

The signatories to an SLA are normally the Service Level Manager and one or more senior User Managers who must represent all the users covered by the SLA. All agreements must be endorsed by the organization's Senior Management.

3.3.6 Availability Manager

The IT Services Manager, or one of his/her staff (again depending on scale) will be designated as 'Availability Manager' and will have overall responsibility for availability of all services running on a system. This will include negotiating and managing the contracts with suppliers which will underpin the SLAs. The Availability Manager is also responsible for ensuring that the availability requirements of new services to be added to existing systems can be met by existing contracts. See the Availability Management module for fuller details of this role.

3.3.7 Capacity Manager

The Capacity Manager has overall responsibility for the capacity and performance of all services and must be closely involved during the formulation of Service Level Requirements to ensure there is adequate IT capacity to meet the required levels of service. Where a new or substantially modified service is to run alongside an existing workload, the Capacity Manager must establish the impact and identify any additional IT capacity required to maintain performance levels. See the Capacity Management module for further details of this role.

3.3.8 Change Manager

Any changes to the system could have implications for service achievement. There is therefore an important need for close liaison with the Change Manager regarding the authorization and timing of all changes.

Brief details of change control procedures must be included in the SLA.

A separate module gives fuller descriptions of the Change Management role.

3.3.9 Others

Network Management, Computer Operations, User Liaison, the Help Desk, Configuration Management, Cost Management, Contingency planning, and optionally Security Management, staff must also be involved in the Service Level Management processes.

3.3.10 Training

The introduction of Service Level Management will result in a significant cultural change for all staff. They will require education and training to adjust to it.

The Service Level Manager and his/her staff may need training to acquire the necessary skills in :

* quality metrics

* performance measurement

* requirement specification

* interpersonal skills

* public speaking

* clear and effective writing.

CCTA are intending to develop training courses aimed at Service Level Managers to cover these matters. Current details can be obtained from the CCTA contact shown in section 9.

3.4 Timing

There are no time constraints preventing the introduction of Service Level Management for existing services, and CCTA strongly recommends that all organizations instigate this as quickly as possible. The preparatory tasks described in this chapter, which must be completed prior to signing of formal agreements, are likely to take anything from 2 to 6 months after the appointment of the Service Level Manager, depending on the size of the organization, the number of agreements, and the support staff available.

Figure 4 shows the steps that must be taken when introducing Service Level Management for a new service, in chronological order. The overall timescale will vary according to the size and complexity of the service, but in all cases the users should be consulted as early as possible to enable them to specify their requirements.

4. Implementation

4.1 Procedures

The Service Level Manager must ensure that the proposed targets are achievable before completing negotiations and signing the formal Service Level Agreements. In the case of existing systems the statistics from the previous 3 months may be used as a basis to establish this, but simple extrapolations based upon current trends may not be adequate to accurately predict performance or response times. It may be necessary to use modelling techniques, as described in the Capacity Management module, to obtain accurate results.

In the case of new systems, where no previous statistics exist, or systems to be modified where previous statistics are inadequate, it is recommended that services are run for a 3 month trial period before SLAs are formally signed. Where achievements fall below expectations, corrective action must be taken, or service levels renegotiated.

When he/she is ready to implement Service Level Management, the Service Level Manager must publish details of the agreements and procedures to be followed to all those staff responsible for the functions described in Figure 5 (Page 22), to the user community, and to all suppliers of underpinning services. Everyone must know how they are affected and any actions they are required to carry out. In particular the users should be reminded that they can now expect to receive consistently good quality IT services as described in the SLAs **provided** they adhere to their side of the agreement and constrain their demands on the service accordingly. Users should also be informed that their day-to-day contact with IT Services, concerning the quality of delivered services should be via the Help Desk.

4.2 Dependencies

Ensure that the dependencies listed in section 3.2 and the contracts shown in Figure 2 (Page 5) are in place prior to implementing Service Level Management.

4.3 People

The Service Level Manager has overall responsibility for ensuring that SLAs are documented and implemented on time.

The central parties to any agreement are obviously the Service Level Manager and the users, but all agreements must be endorsed by the organization's Senior Management.

4.3.1 The help desk

The Help Desk forms the major, and in many cases the only, direct day-to-day contact the Users have with the IT services personnel. Although IT Services will proactively monitor the services for adherence to the SLAs, the Users should be encouraged to contact the Help Desk about any deficiencies in service quality. The Help Desk procedures and efficiency level must be incorporated in the SLAs.

The Help Desk is also involved in smoothing the transition to Service Level Management. The manner in which calls are handled has a significant impact on the Users' perception of the services offered, but this is difficult to legislate for within the SLA. Selection and training of Help Desk personnel is therefore particularly important.

A separate module which gives detailed information about Help Desks is available.

4.3.2 Capacity management

The Capacity Manager has overall responsibility for ensuring that all performance statistics are provided to the Service Level Manager. Many of these will be provided automatically by the system, but specification of monitoring requirements (eg period of snapshots, level of detail etc) must be agreed with the Capacity Manager in advance.

4.3.3 Availability management

The Availability Manager has responsibility for providing availability statistics to the Service Level Manager, but similar considerations apply as in 4.3.2.

4.3.4 Underpinning service suppliers

It will be necessary to negotiate or renegotiate contracts with suppliers of underpinning services (see Figure 2 for details), to ensure that the contracts are sufficiently stringent to support the quality levels agreed in the SLAs. If this involves additional costs the organization must decide whether these costs are justifiable and if not, amend the service level requirements prior to formal signing of the SLAs.

4.3.5 Other support functions

A number of supporting functions, in addition to those described above, will contribute to the effectiveness of Service Level Management. Figure 5 shows those that will be involved.

4.4 Timing

Service Level Management should be implemented as soon as possible. Ensure that the dependencies listed in Section 3.2 and the contracts shown in Figure 2 are in place and are adequate.

5. Post-implementation and Audit

5.1 Procedures

5.1.1 Service level monitoring

A key part of Service Level Management is the monitoring and reporting of the levels achieved, and the comparison of these achievements with the targets set in the SLA. The specific aspects of the service covered by SLAs must be monitored in such a way that an objective view is obtained in order to assess service level achievements. (This will not be possible by merely analysing calls of 'poor response' etc at the Help Desk - although all such calls should obviously be investigated - as such views are often subjective and this method gives no indication of periods when service is good. Users seldom, if ever, ring to report such occurrences). One or more tools, as required, must be used to capture and store accurate service quality details (see Annexes F and G regarding important elements that must be monitored and section 7 for details of tools available).

5.1.2 Daily tasks

On a daily basis, the Service Level Manager must examine the monitoring statistics and Help Desk reports, from the previous working day, to establish service achievements. Where a failure to meet requirements has occurred, or been threatened, an investigation into the cause must be carried out. Any actions necessary to prevent a recurrence of the problem must be initiated. This must involve close liaison with the Problem Manager and the other support functions shown in Figure 5. See also 5.3.

The Service Level Manager must also arbitrate where incidents occur which may impact on service targets, but which could not have been legislated for within the SLAs (eg to decide recovery priorities following a service break, when loss of a software component precludes the normal priority order). Once again this will involve close liaison with other support functions, particularly User Liaison.

5.1.3 Management reporting

Detailed, concise reports must be provided regularly to both users and IT Managers to show the achievements for a particular service.

*   to users - Weekly

*   to the IT Services Managers and appropriate staff - Daily

*   to other IT Managers - Weekly.

Cumulative information must be provided (eg over the last 6-12 months, from beginning of year), in addition to details of yesterday/last week/month.

Comparisons with targets set in the SLA must be included in the reports.

All items within the SLA must be reflected in the reports, typically:

* availability over a measured period, reported as a percentage, together with a measure of unavailability such as service downtime, number of times service down etc

* average peak-hour response time, for the measured period (possibly showing the 95th percentile or picking out typical or particularly important transaction types)

* number of functional errors in each service, reported by level of severity (see Annex G for severity levels)

* the time that each system was operating below the minimum acceptable level of functional anomalies

* average number of users during the peak hour

* peak hour transaction rate for this period

* attempted security violations

* Help Desk call statistics.

5.1.4 Formal review of service quality

The Service Level Manager and User Managers must meet regularly, say monthly, to:

* review service achievements since last meeting

* review service related problems

* identify service trends as they become discernible

* agree minor changes to the service (the Change Management function should be involved)

* initiate any procedural changes (such as re-scheduling workloads, demand management or system tuning) or the preparation of any financial cases required for additional resources, when current service quality is proving unacceptable (this is a 'back-stop': requirements for all resources should generally be foreseen - see 5.1.7).

5.1.5 Non-compliance

Unless the SLA is with a third-party Facilities Management company, it will not be practical to include penalty clauses covering non-compliance. However, whenever a failure to meet requirements does occur, the Service Level Manager and User Managers must jointly analyse the incident, and a full explanation of the cause must be produced, together with proposals for corrective action, whether it be on the part of IT Services or of the users. Wherever negligence or inefficiency is identified, normal management controls must be applied. It is especially important to determine and treat the underlying causes of non-compliances in order to prevent recurrences.

5.1.6 Service improvement programme

A major purpose of Service Level Management is to improve service quality, or maintain existing levels in the face of increasing demand, at minimum cost. To achieve this the Service Level Manager and users must agree a programme of improvements. They must examine recent statistics and identify those aspects of service quality which are causing most concern, or which the users would most like to see improved. The Service Level Manager must then liaise with other IT Services personnel to ensure that resources and effort are targeted accordingly, or cases for additional resources are prepared. Over a period of time this will result in a gradual, steady and affordable improvement in service quality. With the users, the Service Level Manager should proactively seek opportunities for cost-justified service improvements.

5.1.7 Service Level Agreement reviews

SLAs must all be reviewed regularly, at least every six months, in collaboration with the users who were party to the original negotiations (and any others who are appropriate).

The Service Level Manager should examine the SLAs beforehand to plan the changes. Account must be taken of any workload changes identified in past trends or included in any future plans. This information will be necessary to ensure that the service targets will be achievable throughout the lifetime of the SLA. This must be done in conjunction with the Capacity Manager who should, where applicable, use modelling techniques to confirm achievability.

Once agreed with the Users, the original signatories must sign the updated SLAs.

Note! Any change to one SLA could impact on all others. This should be considered during the review.

Amendments to SLAs might be required because of:

* factual amendments, such as new hardware, software or terminals

* amendments due to the above changes, such as the ability to support more users or heavier transaction rates

* new service hours or restrictions etc may be required and negotiated

* more ambitious targets desirable where existing ones are consistently bettered

* growth in transaction levels or business traffic which mean that service quality is no longer acceptable.

The opportunity should be taken for a forward look, over at least a rolling two year period, at service quality, workload and resources requirements. It is particularly important to establish a means of maintaining services levels in the face of workload growth (unless organizations can justify not doing so). This means that any necessary investment in capacity upgrades must be planned well in advance to allow for long lead-times generally associated with hardware procurements.

5.1.8 Underpinning contract reviews

The contracts with suppliers and maintainers of IT infrastructure components should be reviewed regularly, at least every six months, to ensure that they continue to support the users' requirements. Where the review shows that a contract does not fully meet requirements, or cannot continue to meet requirements for the duration of agreements, consideration should be given to re-negotiation.

5.1.9 Reviewing for effectiveness

This sub-section is a checklist for organizations which wish to conduct a management review of the Service Level Management function for effectiveness. It is recommended that such a review is carried out every six months.

Users will only regard the Service Level Management function as effective if all, or at least most, of the following achievements are made:

* the number of incidents when agreed service levels are not provided is very low

* there is a demonstrable reduction in the number of such incidents

* there is a demonstrable reduction in the duration of such incidents

* all issues raised by the users at review times are quickly followed up and resolved.

Records must therefore be examined to ensure these achievements have been made. If they have not been made, the reasons should be recorded.

5.1.10 Auditing for compliance

This sub-section is a checklist for organizations which wish to audit their IT Service Level Management function, using an independent auditor, for compliance to the procedures and advice in this module. It is recommended that such an audit is completed at least annually, and it may be required more regularly, initially or where particular problems are evident.

Checks should be made to ensure that adequate monitoring has been conducted, that accurate reports have been issued in accordance with agreed schedules, and that regular reviews have taken place with the users. These reviews should have been on time, with adequate representation present.

All items raised must have been followed-up and resolved. Evidence that this has occurred must be examined. Verification of user satisfaction will also be necessary.

All documentation should be up-to-date, accurate and complete. The following items must be examined:

* Service Level Agreements

* service achievement records, logs, reports

* review meeting minutes, action records, reports

* standards and procedures documentation.

There are a number of items that can be regarded as milestones, such as:

* completion of new SLA negotiations

* reviews of service achievements

* reviews of SLAs

* production of reports.

Records of each of these must be checked to ensure they were completed accurately and on schedule.

5.2 Dependencies

Tools and procedures must be in place for monitoring, reporting and reviewing service quality. Underpinning contracts shown in Figure 2(Page 5) must be kept under review and maintained up-to-date. Supporting processes shown in Figure 5(Page 22) must be in place.

5.3 People

The Help Desk is responsible for recording, and forwarding to the Service Level Manager, call statistics and details of any incidents which may cause a service target to be threatened or violated.

The Availability Manager is responsible for providing availability statistics. He/she must review the availability achievements and ensure that any actions needed to ensure improvement are carried out. This must involve close liaison with suppliers, and with the Service Level and Problem Managers.

The Capacity Manager is responsible for providing performance statistics. He/she must review performance achievements and recommend any tuning, upgrade or 'demand management' changes needed to restore service levels in liaison with the Service Level, Change and User Managers.

Similarly the Help Desk and Security Managers must review achievements within their province and take any necessary corrective action.

The Service Level Manager, in collaboration with the other managers listed in this sub-section, must analyse all aspects of service achievements and regularly review the results with the User Managers. The Service Level Manager and User Managers must agree any action required where shortfalls occur.

The Change Manager must be fully involved where any changes to the service, or underlying elements, are proposed.

5.4 Timing

Service Level Management must be viewed as a continuing process, and not as a short term solution to a particular problem.

Provide management reports as in paragraph 5.1.3.

Review Service Quality, together with the users, on a monthly basis.

Review Service Level Agreements regularly, at least every six months, and update SLAs accordingly.

Include a forward look at service levels, workloads, and resource requirements spanning a two year window.

Review underpinning contracts regularly, at least every six months, and re-negotiate where appropriate.

Review the effectiveness of the Service Level Management function at least every six months.

Arrange an independent audit of the Service Level Management function for compliance to the procedures and advice contained in this module, at least annually.

6. Benefits, costs and possible problems

This section outlines the benefits and costs of Service Level Management. Some of the benefits, particularly increased user productivity due to improved service quality, will result in large financial savings even where only modest numbers of users are involved. Such saving are likely to significantly outweigh the costs. Organizations should carry out a short cost benefit analysis to establish by how much Service Level Management will be beneficial for them. Consider the existing service levels (the number of service breaks, the time to restore the service, response times etc) and estimate the improvements that will be possible by implementing Service Level Management. Calculate the expected increase in user productivity (eg 5% increase in productivity of 100 users = 5 man years per year x annual staff costs of £15000 = £75000 per year). Balance these savings against expected costs (eg 1 man year per year at £25000 + cost of tools and administration at £15000 = £40000) and calculate the net savings that may be achieved. Also take into account less tangible benefits, such as improved user morale, reductions in the number of disputes etc. In practice it may be possible to redeploy existing staff into Service Level Management.

It is expected that most organizations will calculate a predicted financial benefit from Service Level Management.

6.1 Other benefits

Agreed service levels are vital in stabilizing the relationship between the Service Level Manager and the user:

*   the Service Level Manager becomes responsible for achieving a specific and consistent standard of service which can be measured, providing the User Managers adhere to their side of the agreement(s)

*   the user, in collaboration with IT Services, is able to balance the level of service ostensibly required against the cost and complexity of providing it

*   Service Level Agreements will bring about long term positive cost benefit as a result of the ability to specify more accurately the IT resource actually required

*   Service Improvement Programmes will lead to improved service quality giving increased user productivity

* because the service will be measured objectively, it is likely that any disputes will be resolved more quickly and with less contention

* IT Services are no longer subject to unpredictable demands which make it impossible for them to deliver a 'quality' service

* the agreements will provide an arms length relationship between the users and the providers, which will ease the path to Facilities Management, should it be required

* if organizations base their agreements on the skeleton SLA at Annex B they will be able to use the support tools and training courses which CCTA intends to develop in the future.

6.2 Costs

The costs associated with the implementation of service level management fall into two broad categories:

* the administrative costs of installing and running Service Level Management:

    - the staff costs - estimated at one man-year per year in the average installation, although it may be possible to redeploy existing staff

    - training costs/seminars

    - documentation

* tools required to carry out the process (though some of these tools will also be required for other IT infrastructure management processes).

In addition, Service Level Management may lead to pressure for improved service levels, and these may require additional capital or ongoing expenditure. Organizations should calculate whether these improvements are cost justified. In many cases it is likely that they will be because they will lead to higher user productivity.

6.3 Possible problems

There are a number of possible problems:

* Service Level Management imposes disciplines upon users and IT Services personnel which some may have difficulty accepting. It amounts to a cultural change which 'pins' both sides down. Consistent service quality and mutual understanding will counteract this problem

* it will not be easy for users to decide on their Service Level Requirements and they will require expert assistance from the IT Services Section, who should regard this as part of their normal responsibilities

* the Service Level Manager has the difficult task of costing each proposed level of requirements, but support tools and expert technical backup should help

* automated mechanisms for planning, monitoring and reporting elements of the service are not immediately available for all systems, but CCTA is intending to influence the provision of better support tools

* the Service Level Manager must guard against being over ambitious in agreeing service improvement targets before the necessary planning, monitoring and reporting tools, and underlying procedures, are in place.

Follow the guidelines in this module and ensure targets are realistic.

7. Tools

This section describes the support tools required for Service Level Management, and gives examples of tools currently available. It also gives information on work being carried out by CCTA to stimulate the production of new tools, or improvements to existing tools. The long term aim is to influence the development of integrated support tools to assist all IT Infrastructure Management disciplines, one of which is Service Level Management. This work is a continuing process. Current information can be obtained from the CCTA contact shown in Section 9.

7.1 Monitoring

Most large, modern operating systems provide basic facilities for monitoring system and job activity, transaction processing, network activity, database activity etc. However additional tools are often necessary to integrate and analyse the basic information into a manageable and meaningful format. Examples of this type of tool are BGS's Capture, ICL's VCMS, Carnell's PDR, Sherwood- Computel's VME Monitor and Ultracomp's Sceptre.

A particular problem, however, is that a number of small machines, which are often prominent within distributed or networked systems, lack many or all of the above mentioned facilities. A further problem is that even where tools do exist, they monitor details of the whole system, rather than a specific service that runs on the system. This makes it difficult and time consuming to relate the information provided to specific SLAs. CCTA intends to influence suppliers and software houses to produce new tools, where they do not exist, or amend existing tools to:

* provide data capture facilities for SLAs (based upon the Skeleton SLA at Annex B)

* allow monitoring of individual SLAs

* produce SLA specific reports

* include thresholds and provide alerts when service quality is threatened

* allow pro-active management of service quality.

Early reactions from the trade to these proposals are encouraging.

7.2 Modelling

In order to assess the configuration required to meet the user requirements, and to estimate its costs, a performance/capacity or availability model of the system may be appropriate. These models will also form the basis of continuing Capacity and Availability Management, which are described in separate modules. Examples of performance/capacity modelling tools are BGS's BEST/1 and CRYSTAL, Logica's Capacity/Q, Metron's Athene, ICL's VCSR, and PSI's SCERT II.

SSADM support tools such as CCTA's MUST or LBMS's AUTOMATE+ will provide a valuable source of performance and capacity modelling data. Work is being done by CCTA on developing a direct interface from SSADM to Capacity Modelling tools, and it is hoped that the computer trade will develop tools for this purpose. Metron's Perseus provides an interface from SSADM documentation to Capacity Modelling tools. Later versions will interface to SSADM support tools.

CCTA also hopes to influence the suppliers of Capacity Modelling tools, to widen the scope of their products to include availability and cost modelling, and to better support the Service Level Manager when deciding realistic service targets. Early reaction has again been encouraging.

7.3 Integrated Service Database

An Integrated Service Database, containing all the inventories compiled by the Configuration Management function, and used by Problem Management, Change Management, the Help Desk etc for logging incident details, is an essential source for Service Level Management data. This will also provide the basis for other tools to assist the processes which support Service Level Management. Ideally this database should interface to the Operating System Software, under which the services run. Software packages currently available for IBM, and IBM plug compatible machines which allow some, or all, of these facilities include IBM's INFO/MAN, CA's CA/Netman, and Expertware's CMT/DMT.

Few comparable tools exist for other manufacturers' environments. Fernhart's Service 20, which is primarily a Help Desk tool, provides some of these facilities for ICL VME users, but is not fully integrated into VME. CCTA is hoping to influence a wider availability of such tools across a range of computer manufacturers.

7.4 Accounting

If charging, or notional charging, is implemented, as recommended in this module, then some form of accounting and charging software is essential. The Government Accounting Package (GAP) is available from Carnell Computer Technology (under licence from CCTA) for ICL VME systems, at very low cost for Government users (see Section 9 for details of where further information can be obtained). A number of broadly equivalent packages exist for IBM and IBM Plug-Compatible machines, including Pace's KOMAND III.

7.5 Security

CCTA's Security Methodology CRAMM (CCTA Risk Analysis and Management Methodology) now has an electronic support tool which runs on an IBM PC, or compatible. There is also a comprehensive set of documentation containing advice on IT security entitled Protecting Electronic Information Processing Systems (PEIPS).

Training courses on the topic of IT Security, including CRAMM and PEIPS, are now available through the Civil Service College.

Further details on any of the above subjects, or any other aspect of IT security, are available from:

IT Security and Privacy Group
CCTA
Riverwalk House
157-161 Millbank
London SW1P 4RT
Tel 01-217-3236
GTN 217-3236

7.6 General

More general office software facilities may also be helpful when documenting SLAs, writing reports, or storing relevant data. These will include Word Processing, Spreadsheets, Electronic Mail, Graph Plotting facilities etc.

8. Conclusions and recommendations

Service Level Management is the key to establishing the 'customer/supplier' relationship between the user and the Service Level Manager. The Service Level Agreement provides a specification of the users' expectations and the Service Level Managers' and users' obligations and forms a common agreed basis for measuring the quality of service provided. This will be a long term aid to better management. It will prove cost-effective in reducing the time spent in discussing and resolving conflict between users and IT Services personnel on service levels, when no formal agreement exists.

The main recommendation is that all organizations implement Service Level Management as quickly as practical.

Other recommendations are that:

* the users must be involved as soon as possible in the Service Level Management process

* do not be over ambitious in setting service targets until all the supporting processes and tools are in place

* the skeleton SLA shown at Annex B should be used as a basis for an organization's own agreements

* regular reviews must be conducted to examine the effectiveness of the Service Level Management function, at least every six months

* regular independent audits of the Service Level Management function must be conducted to check for compliance with the procedures and advice contained in this module, at least annually.

9. Further information

Further information on the contents of the module can be obtained from:

CCTA
IT Infrastructure Management Services
Gildengate House
Upper Green Lane
NORWICH
NR3 1DW
Tel: 0603-694617 (GTN 3014-4617).

10. Bibliography

UKCMG Proceedings (annual)

Annex A. Contents of Service Level Agreements

An example Service Level Agreement is shown at Annex B. The structure and detailed content of each SLA will depend on the working practices and requirements of each organization. However it is possible to describe a 'model' set of contents as follows (NOTE! - Only items capable of being measured should be included in the SLA):

* scope of the agreement

* signatories

* date of next review, or period for which the SLA is valid

* dates of previous amendments

Note! - the above 4 items must all appear on the front (title) page

* brief description of service eg:

    - functions

    - applications

    - major transaction types

* service hours:

    - hours for which service is planned to be available (if appropriate, distinguishing between prime shift, maximum support, unattended periods etc)

    - special conditions for week-end, bank holidays etc.

    - relevant notes as to housekeeping, planned maintenance etc

    - details of procedures for requesting changes to the service hours

* service availability:

  - planned percentage availability during service hours

  Note! - Although overall service availability is a valuable indicator, some measure of individual terminal availability, where monitoring facilities allow, may also be valuable (see Annex F for methods of expressing this)

  - maximum number of service failures to be tolerated

  - maximum amount of downtime per failure

  - maximum number of batch jobs that have to be re-run due to error, shown as a percentage of the total (jobs that have been incorrectly submitted should be identified separately)

  - measurement period (eg weekly, monthly, rolling 4-weekly)

  - details of any restrictions or special conditions

  - minimum percentage of terminals available

* user support levels:

  - Help Desk details, including procedures for reporting problems and queries, and Help Desk performance criteria

  - hours when support will be available

  - brief description of support provided

  - user guides; who will have them, distribute them etc.

* performance:

  - target throughput rates; these should be expressed in terms meaningful to the users (eg business transactions rather than TP message-pairs)

  - target response time (possibly subdivided to, say, 70%, 95%, 99% of transactions)

  - target turnaround times

  - measurement period (eg daily, weekly, monthly, rolling 4-weekly)

* details of agreed minimum functionality (see Annex G for guidance on quantifying functionality)

* details of any service charges involved

* change control procedures:

    - brief details of change control procedures

    - details of any planned changes that will impact on the SLA (eg new releases of software, new hardware)

* contingency:

    - brief details of contingency plans in event of major failure etc, including descriptions of essential parts of the service and priorities to aid recovery following such an incident

    Note! - any agreed modifications to the SLA to apply in a contingency situation (eg degraded service, or recovery from total loss of service) must be stipulated.

* anticipated growth:

    in order to assess whether service levels can be maintained for the duration of the agreement it will be necessary to have information about expected growth in business requirements; either new applications or increased transaction rates etc

* restrictions:

    in order to guarantee the agreed levels of service it will be necessary to set a limit on the amount of work that can be accommodated

    - maximum number of transactions

    - maximum number of concurrent logged on users

    - any maximum number of registered users

* central print facilities:

    - hours available

    - printer/stationery types

    - any restrictions

* central print distribution:
  - hours available
  - location of distribution centre
  - description of any postal services
  - any restrictions

* user training:
  - details of training facilities to be made available for users (courses, packages etc) covering both equipment and services

* changes to SLA:

* description of change control procedures for requesting SLA amendments.

Annex B. Skeleton Service Level Agreement

The following document is a skeleton SLA upon which organizations can model their own agreements.This model will also be used as a basis for support tools and training courses which CCTA will be developing in the future. It is therefore recommended that organizations that may wish to use these facilities should use this standard format for their own agreements.

The figures included in the skeleton agreement are examples only and must not be regarded as definitive guidance.

Skeleton Service Level Agreement

This Service Level Agreement is between _____

and_____

The agreement is for the provision of the _____

_____

transaction processing service and associated batch processing, as detailed in later
paragraphs.

This agreement remains valid until superseded by a revised agreement mutually endorsed by
the signatories below. It will be reviewed on a six-monthly basis. Minor changes to the
agreement may be recorded on the form at the end of the agreement providing, once again,
they are mutually endorsed by the two parties.

Service:_____TP Service	Start Date: dd/mm/yy
Service Manager: A.N.Other	Renewal Date: dd/mm/yy

Signatories

Name	Date	Title
A.N.Other	dd/mm/yy	IT Services Manager
A.N.Other	dd/mm/yy	_____Branch Manager

Dates of previous amendments:

_____ _____ _____ _____ _____ _____ _____

_____ _____ _____ _____ _____

Service Description

The _____ Transaction Processing service has the following functions:

_____

_____

_____

The applications running under this service are as follows:

_____   _____

_____   _____

_____   _____

The major transaction types are:

Identity   Description

_____   _____

_____   _____

_____   _____

_____   _____

Service Hours

The service is normally available as follows:

Mon to Thurs-   **08:00hrs to 18:00hrs**

Fri-   **08:00hrs to 16:30hrs**

Special conditions for weekends and bank holidays are as follows:

_____

Pre-scheduled maintenance/housekeeping is carried out on the first Tuesday in every month

but should not impact on the _____ TP service.

The procedures to be followed for requesting changes to the service hours are:

Temporary changes/extensions;_____

_____

Permanent changes;_____

_____

Service Availability

The minimum percentage availability during normal service hours for any user of this service
is **96%**. The average percentage availability for all users is **98%**.

The maximum number of service breaks to be tolerated per rolling 4 week period is **3**.

The maximum time to recover from a service break is **35** mins.

The maximum percentages of batch jobs that have to be re-run due to error are:

Total- **6%**.

Excluding incorrect submissions- **3%**.

The measurement period is a rolling 4 week period.

Details of special conditions are as follows: _____

_____

User support Levels

All problems, queries or requests for assistance must be made to the user Help Desk on Ext. **123**. The Help Desk will be manned from **07:30 to 18:00** each week-day.

Normally calls to the Help Desk must be made only by group liaison officers or their deputies.

Where a problem cannot be immediately resolved the Help Desk staff channel it to the appropriate technical support area. The caller is advised by the Help Desk as soon as a solution is found, or kept informed of progress where appropriate.

Target fault resolution times are as follows:

Severity Level	Times (Hrs)
9	1
8	1
7	1
6	2
5	4
4	8
3	24
2	48
1	at next release
0	at next release

User guide distribution and updating details are as follows_____

_____

Performance

The daily target throughput rates for key transactions are as follows:

Transaction	Rate
_____	**15,000**
_____	**9,000**
_____	**6,500**
_____	**2,000**

The average response times are as follows:

70% of transactions within **2 sec.**

95% of transactions within **3.0 sec.**

100% of transactions within **4.5 sec.**

The average batch turnaround times are as follows:

On-line submission-   **2.5 hr.**

Manual submission-   **6 hr.**

The measurement period is Daily.

Functionality

The agreed minimum level of functionality is as follows (see Annex G for details of suggested severity levels).

No more than the following number of errors per severity level:

Severity Level	Number
9	0
8	0
7	1
6	2
5	3
4	3
3	3
2	6
1	10
0	20

The measurement period is a rolling 4-week period.

Change Control Procedures

Brief details of change control procedures to be followed are as follows;_____

_____

_____

The following planned changes will impact on this agreement;

Change   Date

_____   _____

_____   _____

Contingency

Brief details of contingency plans to be implemented in the event of disaster are as follows:

_____

_____

_____

Security

Security of the system is controlled in accordance with the CRAMM methodology. Any user found guilty of attempting to violate the security of the system will be subject to disciplinary procedures.

Anticipated Growth

The following new application are to be implemented during the lifetime of this agreement:

Application	Anticipated Transaction Rate
_____	2000 per day
_____	800 per day

Increases in transaction rates are expected for the following transaction types:

Application	Anticipated New Rate
_____	1700 per day
_____	600 per day

Restrictions

The performance targets quoted earlier can be achieved only if normal workloads are not heavily exceeded. Degradation is likely to occur if **any** of the following figures are reached:

Maximum transaction rates:

Transaction	Rate
_____	**22,000**
_____	**15,000**
_____	**9,000**
_____	**4,000**
Total	**40,000**

Maximum number of concurrent users - **270**

The following transaction types are not permitted interactively and must be submitted as batch jobs for overnight processing:

_____ _____ _____

_____ _____

Central Print Facilities

Central print facilities are available each day as follows:　　**08:00 to 22:30**

Details of printer and stationery types are as follows:

printers:_____

_____

stationery: _____ _____

_____ _____ _____

_____ _____

Prior arrangements must be made for any job requiring more that **300** sheets of paper, or any special stationery not listed above.

Any jobs waiting to print at the close of the evening shift (22:30) are queued until the following morning, unless special arrangements are made in advance. This may be done as follows:

_____

Central Print Distribution

Print is distributed from the computer centre on an hourly basis, commencing at 08:00 each day, during the following times:

Mon to Thur -	**08:00 to 18:00**
Fri -	**08:00 to 16:00**

Distribution centre points are as follows:

_____ _____ _____

_____ _____ _____

Postal services are available as follows: _____

_____

Any printing completed during the evening is distributed at 08:00 the following morning

unless special arrangements are made in advance. This may be done as follows:_____

_____ _____

Charging

In order to keep user managers informed of resources used by their staff, notional service charges are made and issued to branch management on a monthly basis. Details of the charging formula used are as follows:

_____

_____

Cumulative totals for the financial year and comparative figures for the previous ____ months will also be provided.

Changes to the SLA

Procedures for requesting changes to the SLA are as follows_____

_____

An amendment list for agreed minor changes is attached.

Mandatory renegotiation of the agreement is required if any of the following thresholds are exceeded over 2 consecutive months:

50% increase in average transaction rates

25% increase in number of connected terminals

50% increase in total filestore requirements

Service Reviews

Service review meetings are held at least monthly, where both parties to the agreement will be represented. The purpose of these meetings is to:

*   review service achievements for the previous month

*   identify any specific problems or trends

*   decide upon any actions necessary.

Glossary of terms

Term	Definition / formula
_____	_____
_____	_____
_____	_____

Amendment sheet

Date	Amendment details	Signatories
dd/mm/yy	_____	A. N. Other
	_____	A. N. Other
	_____	
	_____	
dd/mm/yy	_____	A. N. Other
	_____	A. N. Other
	_____	
	_____	
dd/mm/yy	_____	A. N. Other
	_____	A. N. Other
	_____	
	_____	

Annex C. Job Description - Service Level Manager

Main Duties

1. Creates and maintains a catalogue of all existing services offered.

2. Formulates, negotiates and maintains a user/Service Level Agreement structure.

3. Negotiates and agrees the initial contents, and service levels, for each SLA.

4. Analyses and reviews all achieved service levels and conducts comparisons with SLAs.

5. Produces regular reports of service achievements to users and senior management.

5. Chairs monthly meetings with user branch representatives to jointly consider the service levels.

6. Initiates any actions necessary to improve or maintain levels of service.

7. Prepares for and conducts regular reviews of the SLAs with the users, and negotiates and agrees any amendments necessary.

Annex D. Example service catalogue document

Part 1

Service Name: ....   Date: ....

Description: Service type...

                                                 Applications..

                                                 Summary..

                                                 ....

Machine IDs: User ID(s)..

                                                 Job ID(s)..

                                                 File ID(s)..

Scheduling: Anticipated runtimes..............................

                                                 Timing of major events (eg delivery by user etc)
                                                 ....

Inputs: Input documents.....................................

                                                 Data capture requirements...................

Deliverables: Reports...

                                                 time of delivery......................................

                                                 number of copies...................................

                                                 stationery type..

                                                 paper handling requirements..............

                                                 ....

                                                 Tapes...

Dependencies: Input...

                                                 Other services...

                                                 Specific time of day...............................

Assumptions: Descriptions...

Part 2

Service Level
Requirements

Availability...

Service Start/End Times...

Response Times..

Functionality..

Deadlines...

Annex E. Guidance on user/SLA structures

An SLA is a document that can represent the negotiated and agreed set of requirements for either:

* a particular service (a single overall agreement with all users of that service - see Figure 7), or

Figure 7:
Agreement with all
users of a service

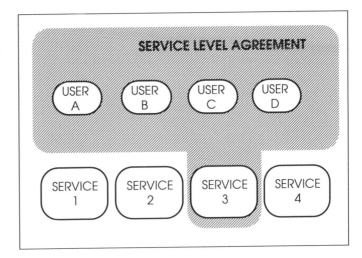

* a particular user, or logical group of users, covering all the services they use, eg a TP Service + 2 Batch services + a Print Service (see Figure 8).

Figure 8:
Agreement with one
user for all services

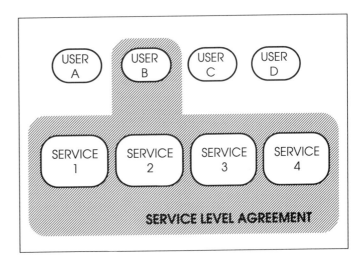

Any combination or variation of the above is permissible to suit particular needs, providing all users and services are covered and there is no overlap.

Decisions on agreement structures are likely to be developed during, or following, the service cataloguing exercise (see section 3.1.1.1).

It is important that all users feel comfortable with their 'fit' into the structure, and that the IT Services section is able to identify clearly and measure all components of each SLA. To achieve this may require an iterative process of negotiations.

Organizations may wish to decide the scope of agreements by using one or more of the following criteria:

*   geographic location

*   business function

*   branch structures

*   ease of monitoring

*   processing mode.

Annex F. Guidance on key service items to be monitored

It is recommended that the following items be monitored (they are of equal relevance to both centralized and distributed systems):

1. Availability and Reliability

*   the achieved overall service availability within contracted service hours

*   the achieved overall service availability within total service hours (this includes contracted hours, plus any extensions)

*   terminal availability (where relevant). This can be monitored at individual terminal level or a formula such as that shown below can be used to produce a single figure giving a broad idea of overall terminal availability

$$\frac{(\text{No.VDUs} \times \text{total mins sched.}) - \text{sum of } (\text{No.VDUs} \times \text{mins down})}{\text{No.VDUs} \times \text{total mins sched.}} \times 100$$

*   the number of service failures

*   the amount of downtime per failure

*   the number of jobs that have to be re-run due to error.

2. Performance

*   response times

*   batch turnaround times

*   throughput rates.

Monitoring tools used must be set up to produce reports reflecting the user/agreement structure to reduce the amount of manual effort involved.

3. Functionality

The functionality of all service aspects must be monitored. See Annex G for guidance on quantifying functionality. All fault reporting mechanisms must include provision for recording levels of severity.

4. Printing/Paper Handling

Records must be kept of all printed output produced and any paper handling work carried out. This will be particularly important where charging algorithms include this effort.

5. Accounting

All IT resources used must be monitored and accounted for, to allow for charging or notional charging. This also provides valuable management information allowing more efficient resource usage.

Annex G. Guidance on quantifying functionality

Regardless of how rigorous Quality Assurance and Testing procedures are, no significant IT system will ever be completely error free. Whenever errors are detected it is important to assess the severity in order to decide what priority and resources, if any, should be allocated to resolving the problem.

All Service Level Agreements must include some agreed minimum level of acceptable functional requirement. In order to achieve this in a quantifiable way some form of severity rating scale must be agreed, resulting in all errors being given a severity 'score'. In the suggested scale shown below the range is 0 to 9, with 9 being most severe. The SLA should include the agreed acceptable number of errors that can be tolerated at each level during the reporting period. All fault reporting mechanisms must include provision for severity levels to be recorded, and these must be monitored, and comparisons must be made with the SLAs.

Suggested Rating Scale

Most severe =

9 Gives wrong results, but no one discovers it right away. By the time it is discovered, there is no way to undo the damage. Issuing duplicate cheques might be an example of this error.

8 Destroys a lot of data, with no way to recover.

7 Destroys data, but can be recovered or re-entered with considerable effort

or

service crashes and the user does not recover within the time period the user would normally expect (needs to be agreed and specified)

or

a legislative change fails to work at all.

6 A feature which used to work, and on which the user has come to depend, fails to work at all

or

the service fails, but it recovers in a normal period of time.

5   A new feature fails to work, but no one is yet dependent on it.

4   A feature is usable, but works differently from its specification, leading to some difficulty in its use.

3   A message to the public contains some major spelling errors, but it is understandable.

2   A message to the user contains some major spelling errors, but it is understandable.

1   A message to the (internal) operator contains some major spelling error, but the message is understandable.

0   There is a very minor difference between the specification and what was developed, but everyone could live with the error indefinitely. For example a spelling error in a message that no one had'ever seen displayed.

Note ! - Any errors not specifically covered on the list must be equated in terms of severity and a 'score' allocated.

The price of this publication has been set to make some contribution to the preparation costs incurred by the department.

Printed in the United Kingdom for HMSO
Dd296907 3/94 C6 G3397 10170

CCTA hopes that you find this book both useful and interesting. We will welcome your comments and suggestions for improving it.
Please use this form or a photocopy, and continue on a further sheet if needed.

From:

        Name

        Organization

        Address

        Telephone

re: 1990/SLM

COVERAGE

Does the material cover your needs?
If not, then what additional material would you like included.

CLARITY

Are there any points which are unclear?
If yes, please detail where and why.

ACCURACY

Please give details of any inaccuracies found.

If more space is required for these or other comments, please continue overleaf.

OTHER COMMENTS

Return to: IT Infrastructure Management Services
Central Computer and Telecommunications Agency
Gildengate House
Upper Green Lane
NORWICH, NR3 1DW